Every Second Something Happens

Poems for the Mind and Senses

Selected by
Christine San José
and
Bill Johnson

Illustrations by Melanie Hall

WORDSONG

Honesdale, Pennsylvania

For the Maples Poetry Posse—grown-ups who can still wonder like children
—C.S.J.

To my wife, Beth, for her love of teaching
—B.J.

Parents and educators: For more information on learning through multiple intelligences, read Howard Gardner's book *Frames of Mind: The Theory of Multiple Intelligences*, published by Basic Books.

Poems written by children courtesy of Highlights for Children, Inc. Copyright © by Highlights for Children, Inc.

Wordsong
An Imprint of Boyds Mills Press, Inc.
815 Church Street
Honesdale, Pennsylvania 18431
Printed in China

Library of Congress Cataloging-in-Publication Data

Every second something happens : poems for the mind and senses / selected by
Christine San José and Bill Johnson ; illustrations by Melanie Hall. — 1st ed.
      p. cm.
  ISBN 978-1-59078-622-2 (alk. paper)
  1. Children's poetry, American. 2. Children's poetry, English. I. San José, Christine.
II. Johnson, Bill. III. Hall, Melanie W., ill.
  PS586.3E94 2009
  811.008'09282—dc22
                              2008024115

First edition
Designed by Tim Gillner and Melanie Hall
The text of this book is set in 13-point Goudy.
The illustrations are done in mixed media.

10 9 8 7 6 5 4 3 2 1

Contents

Imagine That

Wiggle, Waggle, Shimmy, Shake

Love to Share

That's Me!

Acknowledgments

A Note to Parents

Enjoying Poetry Together with Your Child

One summer afternoon, when we were enjoying reading poems to each other that we had newly discovered, we thought: how about a book of little-known gems to share with children? After happy searches through thousands of poems old and new, here is that book. It holds three special delights.

First: fine, fresh, vivid poems.
Say them once, say them twice—saying them together is extra nice. They'll make you laugh, make you sigh, make you imagine, make you ask why.

Second: voices of children among the adults.
Our young poets' views of their world speak directly to young listeners and readers. And the writers' authentic words and images provide reliable models when young readers respond with, "I could write a poem about that!" So keep pencil and paper handy! To the bright senses and inquiring minds of children, every second something happens. How better to capture that than with a poem?

Third: a path into every poem.
We've organized the verse in a way that follows the natural human approaches to making sense of the world: through language, senses (eyes, ears, movement), rational thinking, dealings with others, and knowledge of ourselves. Psychologist and educator Howard Gardner calls these approaches our "intelligences," which we possess in varying degrees and combinations—all of which children surely need to develop as fully as they can.

So this book might quite rightly be reckoned as poetry in the service of children's intellectual development. But we confess that for us it's the other way around: helping children use all their native wits and sensitivities to discover the myriad delights of poetry.

For a good start, you might want to follow the paths suggested by the groupings: finding pictures in the Look at This group of poems, paying attention to sounds in the Listen to This group, and so on. But before long (with little or no prodding), the children will come upon a poem that they realize has too much in it to fit completely into any one group. They will discover that there may well be more than one main path into a poem. So they can find their way in first with pictures, say, but once they are in they can look around for whatever else is there. That's when those varying degrees and combinations of "intelligences" will spark a creative exploration of these fine, fresh, vivid poems.

Enjoy!

Christine San José   *Bill Johnson*

5

Tell Me

Poets choose the very best words

to help us see what they see, hear what they hear, enjoy the stories and jokes that they enjoy, and understand what they think and feel. Poets invite us into their worlds.

Sometimes the voice inviting us is jokey or serious or spooky. Sometimes it's a storyteller's voice. You will find many different voices here, and you can have fun using them when you read the poems aloud. What voices do you think you will use when you write your own poems and read them aloud?

I'm Glad the Sky Is Painted Blue

I'm glad the sky is painted blue,
And the earth is painted green,
With such a lot of nice fresh air
All sandwiched in between.

—*Anonymous*

Baby Brothers

Baby brothers
Have nice little
Kick-a-feet
And little
Clutch-a-hands.

—*Kevin Jones, Age 5*

Little Fish

The tiny fish enjoy themselves
in the sea.
Quick little splinters of life,
their little lives are fun to them
in the sea.

—*D. H. Lawrence*

The Tickle Rhyme

"Who's that tickling my back?" said the wall.
"Me," said a small
caterpillar. "I'm learning
to crawl!"

—*Ian Serraillier*

Six Little Mice

Six little mice sat down to spin;
Kitty passed by and she peeped in.
What are you doing, my little men?
Weaving coats for gentlemen.
Shall I come in and cut off your threads?
No, no, Mistress Kitty, you'd bite off our heads.
Oh, no, I'll not; I'll help you to spin.
That may be so, but you don't come in.

—*Traditional nursery rhyme*

A Sea Serpent Saw a Big Tanker

A sea serpent saw a big tanker,
Bit a hole in her side and then sank her.
It swallowed the crew
In a minute or two,
And then picked its teeth with the anchor.

—*Anonymous*

Summer Twilight

Supper's over
Chores are done
Front porch swims
In setting sun
Rockers beckon
Tea is cold
Children gather
Good as gold
Eight o'clock
The house clocks chime.
Grandpa says:
It's story time.

—Eileen Spinelli

Bobadil

Far from far
Lives Bobadil
In a tall house
On a tall hill.

Out from the high
Top windowsill
On a clear night
Leans Bobadil

To touch the moon,
To catch a star,
To keep in her tall house
Far from far.

—James Reeves

9

A Dream

A dream
is like
a turtle
sleeping peacefully
in a shell.

—*Richie Tran, Age 6*

Night Sky

The sky is not so far away.
It reaches to the ground.
I'm standing right inside of it.
It doesn't make a sound.
And once I almost held a star,
A small and shining light
That turned into a firefly
And flickered out of sight.

—*Margaret Hillert*

"Oh, look!" we say to friends when we spy something interesting or funny or beautiful or perhaps really yucky. These poets are saying, "Oh, look!" They are painting word pictures for us to see with our magical mind's eye. And you might find more than pictures—perhaps sounds, too, or feelings. The closer you look, the more you will find.

Petals gleaming in the sun
And dripping with water in the morning dew,
Sparkling in the rain—
A flower for you!

—*Imogen Hoare, Age 7*

11

A little chipmunk
jumps branch to branch . . . tree to tree.
I watch jealously.

—*Mort Malkin*

Look under the log.
What do you see?
Creepy crawlers coming after me—
big black beetle with claws snapping;
red worms wiggling back and forth;
ants marching in a line,
carrying a load ten times their size.
Hurry! Put the log back.

—*Cade McCoy, Age 9*

Keepers

Well sure it's true
They're not like new,
The soles have worn
A hole or two,

The shine is gone,
The leather's roughed,
The sides are cut,
The toes are scuffed,

One lace is missing,
One's in a knot,
I guess the heels
Don't look so hot,

But otherwise
They're hard to beat,
And I love the way
They fit my feet.

—David L. Harrison

13

Act Fast!

Take down
the picnic umbrella
before the storm,
or, sail-like,
it will fill with wind,
and the USS *Table*
will run aground—
a shipwreck
in a sea of grass.

—*Audrey Baird*

Stories

Only a city
has more stories
behind each windowed
shelf
than a library
can hold
or a storyteller
tell.

—*Allan DeFina*

Mama Bear

Down the valley
where the willows grow
and paintbrush paints
the meadow yellow,
you bring your cubs to breakfast.

The berries are ripe!
Take your time.
Red strawberries
reward the tongue
with sticky sweet jelly.

It's a fine sunny day
to stroll with your cubs,
the sort of day
to lick your lips.
Have another berry.

—David L. Harrison

Undarkening

I am the sun.
I lighten dark spots,
Gazing down at children yelling, screaming.
Old people talk o-o-l-l-d times.
I make the world more pleasant,
I am a symbol of joy,
I kiss you with my gentle rays,
    I am the sun.

—Peter Newcomb, Age 8

Faded

When the light of day
starts to fade away,
when the light in the sky
starts to die,
the little man
who lives in the sun,
never seen
by anyone,
flips off the light—
it's no longer bright.
He shouts to everyone—
"Good night, good night!"

—*Audrey Hockersmith, Age 8*

How far that little candle
  throws his beams!
So shines a good deed
  in a naughty world.

—*William Shakespeare*

Listen to This

What sounds do you hear

when you wake up in the morning? What *bing-bang-booms* during the day? What singsong murmurs as you drift off to sleep? Do you like making noises? *Shh* now—can you hear your own breathing? All those sounds you hear—they'd make a poem just listing them! In this section, you'll find that the "listen!" poems ask to be read aloud. There's a hushed one, a singsong one, one to chant . . .

Wind

Wind tickles my nose
   and whispers to me
soft secrets from
far away.

—*Taylor Johnson, Age 8*

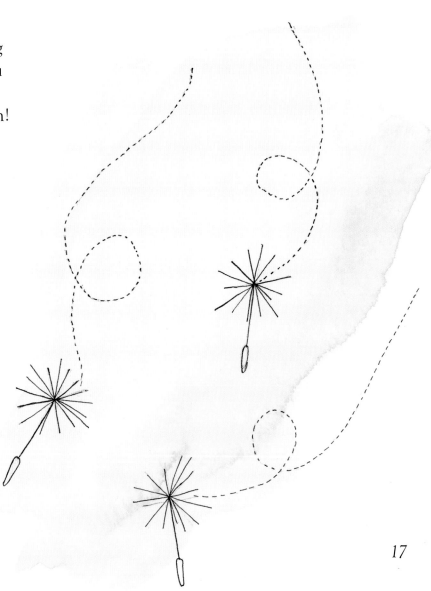

Evening

A sherbet sky,
sun setting slow.
A porch swing creaking
to and fro.
A mother singing
sweet and low.
A baby nodding—
off he goes.

—Ashley Brown, Age 11

Cradle Song of the Elephants

The little elephant was crying
because it did not want to sleep . . .
Go to sleep, my little elephant,
the moon is going to hear you weep.

Papa elephant is near.
I hear him bellowing among the mangoes.
Go to sleep, my little elephant,
the moon will hear my little fellow . . .

—Adriano del Valle
(Brazilian poem translated by Alida Maikus)

18

Table Manners

The Goops they lick their fingers,
  And the Goops they lick their knives;
They spill their broth on the tablecloth—
  Oh, they live disgusting lives!
The Goops they talk while eating,
  And loud and fast they chew;
And that is why I'm glad that I
  Am not a Goop—are you?

—*Gelett Burgess*

Wild Geese

Wedges of wild geese overhead
Send their honking down on us.
The way they carry on up there
Makes me think one missed the bus.

—*Dawn Watkins*

Sea Speak

If every ocean
and every sea
held an intercoastal
spelling bee,
with all the surf
from far and near,
these are some
of the words we'd hear:
thundering
whacking
smacking
splashing
lashing
slapping
lapping
licking
tickling
gurgling
spurting
spritzing
pounding . . .
and the sound
of that oh-so-gentle inhalation:
froooosh!

—Bobbi Katz

Baby's Drinking Song

Sip a little
Sup a little
From your little
Cup a little
Sup a little
Sip a little
Put it to your
Lip a little
Tip a little
Tap a little
Not into your
Lap or it'll
Drip a little
Drop a little
On the table
Top a little.

—James Kirkup

Beneath the Moon

Beneath the moon there is a hill
And in that hill there is a hall
And in that hall there is a throne
And on that throne there sits a king
And in his hand a crystal ball
And in that ball there shines a moon
And beneath that moon there is a hill
And in that hill there is a hall
And in that hall there is a throne
And on that throne . . .

—*Mike Harding*

The House in Winter

Is anything as quiet
As a night of snow?
"I don't know.
If you don't think about
The way a house will snap,
And how the pines blow,
And the wind roars
Under the shutters
And makes them flap.
Or how the gust
Down the chimney flutters
Like a bat that wants out,
Or about the creaky floors,
I guess you could just
About say it was quiet."

—*Dawn Watkins*

Time to put on your thinking cap!

You'll need it for counting, for solving riddles, for wondering at the many marvels in the world, another for imagining, another for seeing things from somebody else's point of view. You'll find all of those things to think about here.

Every Second Something Happens

Every second someone is DEAD.
Every second someone is BORN.
Every second there is a CRASH.
Believe me,
Every second something happens.

—Sam Wamack, Age 6

If You Should Fall, Don't Forget This

Someone big and someone small
Tripped and banged their heads on the wall.

Someone small got a little bump.
But someone big got a great big lump!

There is one good thing about being small—
You just don't have so far to fall.

And here's another—when you do,
You have less to pick up. Now isn't that true?

—John Ciardi

Royal Riddle

What inched along like a furry worm?
What thought of flying but could only squirm?
What made a case as clear as glass,
And hung it on a stalk of grass?
What went to sleep a dull, slow thing,
And woke to find himself a king?*

—Dawn Watkins

* a monarch butterfly

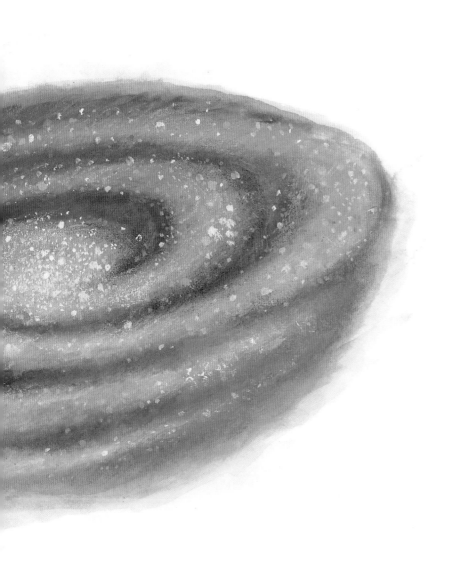

The Countless Stars

Suppose you stood
on a darkened slope
and looked at the sky
through a telescope
and counted the stars
for hours . . . or, say,
you counted a night
of your life away . . .

You'd just make a *start*,
a very small try,
at counting the number
of stars in the sky.

—*Aileen Fisher*

Shadow

My shadow is hiding
In the darkness.
The moon will give it back to me,
Because it's so bright.

—*Ted Schroeder, Age 2*

Softer than a moth's wing,
Lighter than a sigh,
Who was it
And
What was it
That just went by?

—*Ivy O. Eastwick*

26

Hippo Kisses

A hippo's lips are two feet wide;
So if he wants to kiss you,
He has to kiss you up the side—
Or his kiss will mostly miss you.

—*Dawn Watkins*

The Fishing Trip

I can do a lot of things
A fish can't.
For instance, I can whistle, but
A fish can't,
And I can multiply by two's,
Read a book and tie my shoes
And know which spoon or fork to use, which
A fish can't.
Compared to fish it's safe to say
I'm better and smarter in every way,
But I tried to catch a fish today, and
I can't.

—*David L. Harrison*

27

The Prayer of the Little Ducks Who Went into the Ark

Dear God,
Give us a flood of water.
Let it rain tomorrow and always.
Give us plenty of little slugs
and other luscious things to eat.
Protect all folk who quack
and everyone who knows how to swim.
                                        Amen.

—Carmen Bernos de Gasztold
   (Portuguese poem translated by Rumer Godden)

The Cat and the Goldfish

In the bowl, the goldfish sat.
Slyly creeping, came the cat.
Splishy! Splashy! Gobble! Crunch!
The goldfish ate the cat for lunch!

—Joy Cowley

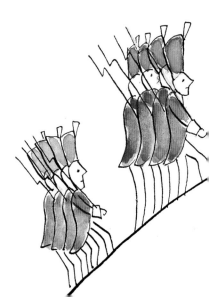

Here's a marching poem,

a squishing poem, a flying poem, a fast-and-slow poem, a slinky poem, a thumping poem—so jump in! Can you move like the words in the poems while you're saying them? If you can, we're sure the poet would shout with delight, "Way to go!"

The Brave Old Duke of York

Oh, the brave old Duke of York,
  He had ten thousand men;
He marched them up to the top of
    the hill,
  And he marched them down again.
And when they were up, they were up,
  And when they were down, they
    were down,
And when they were only halfway up,
  They were neither up nor down.

—*Anonymous*

29

Beetle

Beetle, Beetle,
why so fast?

Out of my way!
I must get past!

Beetle, Beetle,
where do you run?

Away from Lizard
and out of the sun.

Beetle, Beetle,
what will you do?

I'll drink a drop
of morning dew.

—David L. Harrison

30

Football

Spins
like a rocket
traveling through the air
twirling just right
slow twisting
CATCH!
GOOD THROW!

—*Adam Kriegshauser, Age 6*

Mud

I like mud.
I like it on my clothes.
I like it on my fingers.
I like it in my toes.

Dirt's pretty ordinary
And dust's a dud.
For a really good mess-up
I like mud.

—*John Smith*

Alley Cat

A bit of jungle in the street
He goes on velvet toes,
And slinking through the shadows stalks
Imaginary foes.

—*Esther Valck Georges*

The Intruder

Two-boots in the forest walks,
Pushing through the bracken stalks.

Vanishing like a puff of smoke,
Nimbletails flies up the oak.

Longears helter-skelter shoots
Into his house among the roots.

At work upon the highest bark,
Tapperbill knocks off to hark.

Painted-wings through sun and shade
Flounces off along the glade.

Not a creature lingers by,
When clumping Two-boots comes to pry.

—*James Reeves*

To a Playful Kite

Fly
high,
dance
with the wind,

Gliding,
flipping
in the sky,

Prancing,
dancing
over the world,
lunging at the
trees,

Like a friend
playing
with me.

—*Joey Lyon, Age 11*

Leaf Birds

Fly, leaves, fly
From your maple tree.
Dive, leaves, dive
Down to play with me.
Rise, leaves, rise
When I throw you high.
Fly like birds
Closer to the sky.

—*Travis Bronson, Age 7*

33

I Am the Earth

I am a red apple in a tree.
I am a robin singing in the sky.
I am a tapping noise of the rain.
I am a horse running free.
I am a shooting star in the night.
I am snow falling from the sky.

I am the Earth. I am alive.

—*Kyle Marra, Age 7*

A Circle of Sun

I'm dancing.
I'm leaping.
I'm skipping about.
I gallop.
I grin.
I giggle.
I shout.
I'm Earth's many colors.
I'm morning and night.
I'm honey on toast.
I'm funny.
I'm bright.
I'm swinging.
I'm singing.
I wiggle.
I run.
I'm a piece of the sky
in a circle of sun.

—*Rebecca Kai Dotlich*

Love to Share

Feelings of love are hugely important to us all. So here you'll find poems about people—family and friends—who live in a special place in your heart. And next time you want to give someone a present, guess what you could roll up and tie with a ribbon? How wonderful if it's written by you.

Love

If I was a turtle
I would make ripples in a silver pond
And they would come out gold
Just for you.

—Lisa DiMatteo, Age 7

My Natural Mama

my natural mama
is gingerbread
all brown and
spicy sweet.
some mamas are rye
or white or
golden wheat
but my natural mama
is gingerbread,
brown and spicy sweet.

—*Lucille Clifton*

Marriage

I'm marrying Masashi—
because I like him.
Ryoko is marrying Yū.
The girls
all know who
but the boys
don't know at all.

—*Tezuka Maiko, kindergarten*

My Mom and Dad

I snuggle up to them when I'm scared.
I kiss them and hug them with joy and happiness.
I cry in their arms when I'm sad.
How I love my mom and dad.

—*Allison Salmon, Age 8*

A father is a man
Who is waiting to be
A grandpa, which is
A child's best friend.

—Alison Aubrecht, Age 9

Grandmothers

When you have a problem
tell your grandmother.
She will take a part
from her heart
for you.

—Danielle Sanchez, Age 9

It's Me . . . Grandma . . . It's Me

Sometimes Grandma
Forgets my name.
I don't know why.
It's still the same.

When she does,
I whisper low,
"It's me . . . Mary Ellen . . .
And I love you so."

—Mary Ellen Pruitt

My Grandad

His eyes as bright as the deep blue sea,
And his smile as big as a pot of gold,
His face as nice as the morning dew,
I used to tell him, "I love you!"

Grandma was so nice to him,
It gave him a smiling grin.
Now he is free from being ill.
You know, Grandad, I love you still.

—Taylor Zediker, Age 5

Lullaby

It is my big baby
That I feel in my hood
Oh how heavy he is!
Ya ya! Ya ya!

When I turn
He smiles at me, my little one,
Well hidden in my hood,
Oh how heavy he is!
Ya ya! Ya ya!

How sweet he is when he smiles
With two teeth like a little walrus.
Ah, I like my little one to be heavy
And my hood to be full.

—*Thule Eskimo*

My Aunt Sue

My Aunt Sue, tall and graceful
as a bamboo,
bends to weed her garden bed,
talks to pansies, pinks, and me
under warm skies.

Braiding her white halo,
she teaches me
to make ixora beads
brightening my old shirt like
a party dress.

In her garden we watch insects
curl in buttercups.
Morning glories open at dawn.
Sunflowers turn to the sun.
My world grows with Aunt Sue.

—*Monica Gunning*

The Power of Two

If I wish
and
You wish
the
same wish
at the
same time
not
an hour
or
a minute
or
a second
apart

Then
the wish
that
I wish
and
You wish
will
become
one wish
with the
power
of two

—*Elizabeth Fein, Age 11*

Who is that person in the mirror?

What does that person think and feel? What does that person want to do—now? Next year? In ten years? In these poems, there's something to learn about other people as they look in their own mirror. What do you find when you look into your own heart? Whatever it is, keep that last little poem in this book inside your head and heart. The poet wrote it for herself—and for all of us.

Today is my last day of being five.
I have one more day to think fively thoughts.

—*Olivia Smith, Age 5*

My Book!

I did it!
I did it!
Come and look
At what I've done!
I read a book!
When someone wrote it
Long ago
For me to read,
How did he know
That this was the book
I'd take from the shelf
And lie on the floor
And read by myself?
I really read it!
Just like that!
Word by word,
From first to last!
I'm sleeping with
This book in bed,
This first FIRST book
I've ever read!

—David L. Harrison

Reflections

What is this I see
staring up at me,
a person
in the water?
A small,
   pale,
   delicate,
familiar person.
   I know her;
for it is only me,
only me that I see.
Rain has started;
where it was once
glassy pools of my reflections
is ruffled mirrors of waves.
The girl has faded,
and I trudge on
through the puddle
where the girl once was . . .

—Shannon Coffey, Age 13

If I frown
and turn
upside down . . .
I'm smiling.

—*Alyssa Van Thoen, Age 6*

Pout

No use
acting nice to me
when I'm stuck
in a pout.
I can't let your
niceness in
until my mad
wears
out.

—*Sara Holbrook*

Feelings

When you are calm
you are like a flowing stream.
When you are sad
you are like a lonesome hooting owl.
When you are angry
you are like a rushing river.
When you are happy
you are like a flying bird.

—*Jaimie Gomes, Age 8*

Wild Geese

I heard the wild geese flying
In the dead of the night,
With beat of wings and crying
I heard the wild geese flying.

And dreams in my heart sighing
Followed their northward flight.
I heard the wild geese flying
In the dead of the night.

—*Elinor Chipp*

44

When I Grow Up

Ballerinas stand on their toes
I'm going to grow up
and be one of those.

—*Michelle Lea Griffith, Age 5*

I Want to Be

When I grow up,
Got a lot of things
I want to be.
So I want to hurry up
And grow up.
I want to be a teacher
And teach the children of the world,
I want to be an artist
And paint the beauty of the world,
I want to be a doctor
And treat the people of the world,
I want to be a cook
And cook the food of the world,
I want to be a newsman
And report the news of the world,
I want to be myself
And there's nobody in the world
Like me.

—*Frank Yazzie, Age 10*

Proud

I am the flying bird,
I am the flowing water,
I am the burning sun in the sky,
I am the wild rose,
the speeding cheetah,
I am the tall trees in the wood,
I am the dragon soaring
and the eagle's spirit.
I am me and I am
proud.

—Heather Nicholson, Age 11

46

I will walk the way I walk
I will talk the way I talk
I will see the way I see
And take pleasure being me.

—*Jolyn Thomason*

Acknowledgments

Every possible effort has been made to trace the ownership of each poem included in *Every Second Something Happens: Poems for the Mind and Senses*. If any errors or omissions have occurred, corrections will be made in subsequent printings, provided the publisher is notified of their existence.

BJU Press for "Hippo Kisses," "Royal Riddle," and "Wild Geese" by Dawn Watkins. Copyright by BJU Press, Greenville, South Carolina. Used with permission.

Bobbi Katz for "Sea Speak" from *A Rumpus of Rhymes: A Book of Noisy Poems* by Bobbi Katz, published by Dutton Children's Books, New York. Copyright © 2001 by Bobbi Katz. Used with permission of the author who controls all rights.

Boyds Mills Press for "Act Fast!" from *Storm Coming!* by Audrey B. Baird. Copyright © 2001 by Audrey B. Baird; "Beetle" from *Farmer's Garden* by David L. Harrison. Copyright © 2000 by David L. Harrison; "A Circle of Sun" from *Lemonade Sun* by Rebecca Kai Dotlich. Copyright © 1998 by Rebecca Kai Dotlich; "The Countless Stars" from *Sing of the Earth and Sky* by Aileen Fisher. Copyright © 2001 by Aileen Fisher; "If You Should Fall, Don't Forget This" from *You Know Who* by John Ciardi. Copyright © 1964 by John Ciardi. Copyright renewed 1991 by Judith H. Ciardi; "Keepers" from *The Alligator in the Closet* by David L. Harrison. Copyright © 2003 by David L. Harrison; "Mama Bear" from *Wild Country* by David L. Harrison. Copyright © 1999 by David L. Harrison; "My Book!" from *Somebody Catch My Homework* by David L. Harrison. Copyright © 1993 by David L. Harrison; "Night Sky" from *The Sky Is Not So Far Away* by Margaret Hillert. Copyright © 1996 by Margaret Hillert; "Pout" from *I Never Said I Wasn't Difficult* by Sara Holbrook. Copyright © 1996 by Sara Holbrook; "Stories" from *When a City Leans Against the Sky* by Allan A. De Fina. Copyright © 1997 by Allan A. De Fina; "Summer Twilight" from *Tea Party Today* by Eileen Spinelli. Copyright © 1999 by Eileen Spinelli.

Lucille Clifton for "My Natural Mama" by Lucille Clifton from *Poems for Mothers*. Copyright © 1988. Published by Holiday House. Reprinted by permission of Curtis Brown, Ltd.

Monica Gunning for "My Aunt Sue" by Monica Gunning. Copyright © 1993 by Monica Gunning.

Mike Harding for "Beneath the Moon" from *Up the Boo Aye Shooting Pookakies* by Mike Harding. Copyright Mike Harding.

David L. Harrison for "The Fishing Trip" by David L. Harrison.

Highlights for Children, Inc., for "The House in Winter" by Dawn Watkins; "Softer than a moth's wing" by Ivy O. Eastwick; "The Cat and the Goldfish" by Joy Cowley; "It's Me … Grandma … It's Me" by Mary Ellen Pruitt.

Mort Malkin for "A little chipmunk" by Mort Malkin.

Bruno Navasky for "Marriage" by Tezuka Maiko from *Festival in My Heart*. Copyright © 1993. Published by Harry N. Abrams, Inc. Translated by Bruno Navasky.

Pollinger Limited and the Estate of Frieda Lawrence Ravagli for "Little Fish" from *The Complete Poems of D. H. Lawrence* by D. H. Lawrence. Permission granted by Pollinger Limited and the Estate of Frieda Lawrence Ravagli.

Jolyn Thomason for "I Will Walk" by Jolyn Thomason.